The **INSIDE** **GUIDE**

DOCUMENTS OF DEMOCRACY

The Declaration of Independence

By Sadie Silva

Cavendish Square

New York

Published in 2022 by Cavendish Square Publishing, LLC
29 East 21st Street, New York, NY 10010

First Edition

Website: cavendishsq.com

This publication represents the opinions and views of the author based on his or her personal experience, knowledge, and research. The information in this book serves as a general guide only. The author and publisher have used their best efforts in preparing this book and disclaim liability rising directly or indirectly from the use and application of this book.

All websites were available and accurate when this book was sent to press.

Portions of this work were originally authored by John Shea and published as *The Declaration of Independence* (*Documents That Shaped America*). All new material this edition authored by Sadie Silva.

Library of Congress Cataloging-in-Publication Data

Names: Silva, Sadie, author.
Title: The Declaration of Independence / Sadie Silva.
Description: New York : Cavendish Square Publishing, [2022] | Series: The
inside guide: documents of democracy | Includes bibliographical
references and index.
Identifiers: LCCN 2020042254 | ISBN 9781502660329 (library binding) | ISBN
9781502660305 (paperback) | ISBN 9781502660312 (set) | ISBN
9781502660336 (ebook)
Subjects: LCSH: United States. Declaration of Independence–Juvenile
literature. | United States–Politics and
government–1775-1783–Juvenile literature.
Classification: LCC E221 .S495 2022 | DDC 973.3/13–dc23
LC record available at https://lccn.loc.gov/2020042254

Editor: Caitie McAneney
Copyeditor: Jill Keppeler
Designer: Jessica Nevins

Some of the images in this book illustrate individuals who are models. The depictions do not imply actual situations or events.

CPSIA compliance information: Batch #CW22CSQ: For further information contact Cavendish Square Publishing LLC, New York, New York, at 1-877-980-4450.

Printed in the United States of America

Find us on

CONTENTS

The Declaration of Independence, along with the U.S. Constitution, is one of the founding documents of the United States.

A ROCKY RELATIONSHIP

*I*n 1607, England established its first permanent settlement in North America at Jamestown, Virginia. More people then began arriving in the New World to establish colonies for England. For more than 100 years, the British government and its American colonies had a fairly good relationship. However, in 1776, those colonies issued the Declaration of Independence, formally breaking away from Britain. What went wrong?

The British Colonies

For many years, the British government rarely interfered in the daily lives of American colonists. Between the 17th and 18th centuries, 13 British colonies were established: Virginia, New York, New Hampshire, Massachusetts, Maryland, Connecticut, Rhode Island, Delaware, North Carolina, South Carolina, New Jersey, Pennsylvania, and Georgia. The colonies' governing bodies made most of their laws.

Colonies weren't supposed to trade with other countries or manufacture certain goods. Their only option for some goods was to buy British ones. This played into a system called mercantilism, which benefited the British. In exchange, the British army and navy protected American lands and ships. Despite the thousands of miles separating the two lands, most American colonists still considered themselves British citizens. It wasn't until the 1750s that things started to change.

Fighting the French and Indian War

The French and Indian War was a turning point in the relationship between Britain and its American colonies. Between 1754 and 1763, the British and French battled for control of vast areas of North America.

The French and Indian War was fought on American soil between Britain and France, along with their Native American allies.

King George III ruled England for nearly 60 years. While he was successful in winning the Seven Years' War, he lost his American colonies in the American Revolution.

Many colonists didn't care about the war, thinking it was England's conflict and not theirs. Others wanted to be able to defend their lands from the French. They asked for the British government's permission to raise an American army. King George III wouldn't allow it. Instead, colonists were asked to fight with the British army, and thousands did. However, many were kept from holding high-ranking positions, insulted, and sometimes even sent home by British officers. The British won the French and Indian War, but its effects were long-lasting as colonists began to question British rule.

George Washington served in the British army in the French and Indian War. Later, he was the commander in chief of the Continental Army during the American Revolution.

THE QUARTERING ACT

British soldiers didn't leave North America after the French and Indian War ended. Some stayed to patrol the land won from the French. The Quartering Act of 1765 stated that colonists had to provide food, shelter, and supplies to the British forces. This later shaped the U.S. Constitution, as shown in Third Amendment (part of the Bill of Rights). This amendment, or change to the document, bans the peacetime quartering, or housing, of soldiers in someone's house without the owner's permission. In wartime, quartering would require special laws. The presence of soldiers had made colonists feel tense, so the **Founding Fathers** didn't want to repeat history.

British military presence in Boston, Massachusetts, angered colonists there. During the Boston Massacre on March 5, 1770, soldiers opened fire on a group of angry colonists, killing five.

Taxation Without Representation

The French and Indian War left England with a considerable amount of debt, or money owed. In fact, England's debt almost doubled from 1755 to 1764. Since the war was fought in North America, the British thought the American colonies should help pay for it. British citizens in England were so heavily taxed the government was concerned they might rise up in the face of more taxes. Their solution to this problem was **imposing** taxes on colonists for necessary goods.

In 1764, the British introduced the Sugar Act, which imposed a tax on sugar, molasses, and other goods. The following year, Britain passed the Stamp Act, and others quickly followed.

"No taxation without representation" became a rallying cry among American protesters. Many colonists weren't just angry about costly taxes. They also felt it was unjust to have decisions made an ocean away, without their input. Many people believed it was time for a change. These feelings became the basis for a document that changed the world: the Declaration of Independence.

This illustration shows colonists protesting the Stamp Act in New York in 1765.

The Boston Tea Party was a colonial act of protest against the British Tea Act. Colonists dressed as Native Americans and dumped crates of tea into Boston Harbor.

THE ROAD TO REVOLUTION

Colonists began to protest British actions. For example, in response to increasing taxes on imported goods, groups of women helped organize **boycotts**. Instead of buying British goods, such as clothing, the Daughters of Liberty made their own. Protests such as boycotts and the Boston Tea Party helped colonists realize their power. They were starting down the path that would lead to the Declaration of Independence.

Punishing Protesters

Britain didn't take kindly to colonial protests. Instead of listening to colonial calls for change, Britain took more control over the American colonies. When the New York colonial assembly voted not to obey the Quartering Act, the British disbanded, or broke up, the assembly. After the Boston Tea Party, King George III limited the powers of the government of Massachusetts as well.

The actions King George III took to punish the colonies of New York and Massachusetts were meant to discourage other colonies from disobeying British authorities. However, they had the opposite effect; colonists in other places felt sympathy for those in New York and Massachusetts and became angry with the British government.

The First Continental Congress met in Carpenters' Hall in Philadelphia, Pennsylvania.

In September 1774, representatives from every American colony except Georgia formed the First Continental Congress to discuss what to do next. This meeting of colonial representatives sparked a revolution.

Fighting Breaks Out

Revolutionary **militias** began to form in Massachusetts in response to increased British presence. Militias started gathering weapons, which prompted British troops to march to Concord, Massachusetts. Part of the British plan was to arrest revolutionary leaders Samuel Adams and John Hancock. Luckily, they were warned and escaped. However, colonial militiamen and British soldiers clashed at the Battles of Lexington and Concord on April 19, 1775.

THE FIRST CONTINENTAL CONGRESS

The First Continental Congress was made up of 56 delegates from 12 colonies. They met in Carpenters' Hall in Philadelphia, Pennsylvania, between September 5 and October 26, 1774. The purpose of the Congress was to show a united front in dealing with England, even though the colonies weren't united at all. Some wanted peace with England, others wanted more colonial rights, and still other colonies wanted complete separation. They did agree that the first step was to inform the king of the colonies' concerns. In October 1774, the Congress sent a letter to King George III stating their **grievances**. They also organized a boycott of British goods.

Fast Fact

The First Continental Congress was a response to the Coercive Acts, also called the Intolerable Acts. They established military rule in Massachusetts, among other injustices.

Members of the colonial militia were also called minutemen because they claimed to be ready to fight the British at a minute's notice.

To this day, no one knows which side fired the first shot of the war. Although they were outnumbered at first, several hundred colonists joined the battle and forced the most powerful army in the world to retreat. The fighting of the American Revolution had begun.

The Second Continental Congress

The Battles of Lexington and Concord raised tensions even higher in the colonies. Delegates decided to meet again in May 1775 as part of the Second Continental Congress. This Congress prepared for war with the British. They formed the Continental Army, and they appointed George Washington as its leader.

However, many of the delegates still hoped for peace. In July 1775, they wrote the Olive Branch Petition, which pleaded with King George III to stop taking action against the colonies. Again, Congress stated the colonies' loyalty to their king.

The Olive Branch Petition was created in July 1775 by the Second Continental Congress. It listed grievances and declared the rights of the colonies.

24

To the King's Most Excellent Majesty.

Most Gracious Sovereign!

We your Majesty's faithful Subjects of the colonies of New-Hampshire, Massachusetts-Bay, Rhode-Island and Providence Plantations, Connecticut, New-York, New-Jersey, Pensylvania, the Counties of New-Castle, Kent and Sussex on Delaware, Maryland, Virginia, North-Carolina, and South-Carolina in behalf of ourselves and the inhabitants of those colonies who have deputed us to represent them in General Congress, by this our humble petition, beg leave to lay our grievances before the throne.

King George refused to read the Olive Branch Petition. When news of this rejection reached the colonies, it changed the opinion of many Americans. They began to see King George as a **tyrant**. The Second Continental Congress had a new goal in mind—independence.

John Hancock was president of the Second Continental Congress. He signed his name in large letters on the Declaration of Independence.

The Committee of Five (Roger Sherman, Robert Livingston, John Adams, Benjamin Franklin, and Thomas Jefferson) was selected to write the Declaration of Independence.

E ven those who had been loyal to Britain started to call for independence. Now it was the job of the Second Continental Congress to draw up an official document. The result was the Declaration of Independence, which had three major parts: a preamble, a list of grievances, and a formal statement that declared independence.

Fast Fact

On June 7, 1776, Virginia delegate Richard Henry Lee proposed "that these United Colonies are, and of right ought to be, free and independent States."

The Preamble

The preamble opens the document. It begins, "When in the course of human events, it becomes necessary for one people to dissolve the political bands which have connected them with another … " In writing this,

Robert Livingston was on the Committee of Five tasked to write the Declaration of Independence. However, he was called to New York before he could sign it.

Thomas Jefferson was the main author of the Declaration of Independence. Later, he served as the third president of the United States.

Thomas Jefferson was proposing that it was "necessary" for Americans to have independence.

Jefferson identified Americans as "one people" and the British as "another." In doing so, Jefferson was suggesting that the colonists weren't British citizens anymore. This was important to other countries that wouldn't want to get involved in a British **civil war**.

Perhaps the most famous line of the Declaration of Independence reads, "We hold these truths to be self-evident, that all men are created equal, that they are endowed by their Creator with certain unalienable Rights, that among these are Life, Liberty and the pursuit of Happiness." Jefferson followed this with a call to "alter or **abolish**" any government that went against these basic human rights.

A List of Grievances

The longest section of the Declaration of Independence is the list of grievances, which proves why it was necessary to overthrow the unjust government. Jefferson began the list of grievances with the shortest sentence in the Declaration: "To prove this, let Facts be submitted to a candid world." Jefferson called his points "Facts," not disagreements or opinions, and he directed those facts not only to the British government, but also to the wider world.

INSPIRATION FOR THE DECLARATION

Thomas Jefferson was the primary author of the Declaration of Independence, and his sources of inspiration were clear. He borrowed ideas from English **Enlightenment** philosopher John Locke. Locke's contract theory of government stated that governments' powers came from the consent of the people.

Some of Jefferson's ideas in the preamble of the Declaration of Independence were influenced by an important document from his home state: the Virginia Declaration of Rights. The Declaration of Rights also stated the belief that all men have freedoms that cannot be taken away, including the rights to life, liberty, and the pursuit of happiness. These ideas of equality and **democracy** shine through Jefferson's writing.

This illustration imagines Thomas Jefferson drafting the Declaration in Independence by candlelight from a boarding house in Philadelphia.

Grievances included the king's interference with colonial governments and his army's occupation of colonial land during peacetime. Jefferson also listed taxation without consent, the prevention of trade with other countries, and disregard for the colonists' right to a trial by jury. The document accused the British ruler of waging a war on his own colonies.

Jefferson also pointed out that the British government and people didn't protest on behalf of the colonies when King George carried out unfair measures against them. Because of these grievances, therefore, the colonies had a right to declare independence.

Declaring Independence

The final section of the Declaration of Independence states the next step the colonies wanted to take. It reads, "These United Colonies are, and of Right ought to be Free and Independent States."

Several important points are made in this section. First, the Declaration broke all ties with the

Benjamin Franklin was a printer, inventor, scientist, writer, Founding Father, and part of the Committee of Five in charge of the Declaration.

British government. Next, the colonies asserted they had the right to wage war and declare peace. Third, the document established that the

new United States could form alliances with other countries. Finally, Americans declared that they had "full Power … to do all other Acts and Things which Independent States may of right do."

The Declaration was an incredible risk. The new states still had to win the American Revolution against the full weight of the British military. They had to show a united front, and so the document concludes with: " … we mutually pledge to each other our Lives, our Fortunes and our sacred Honor."

This illustration shows Benjamin Franklin during his time in France. He traveled there to win support for American independence.

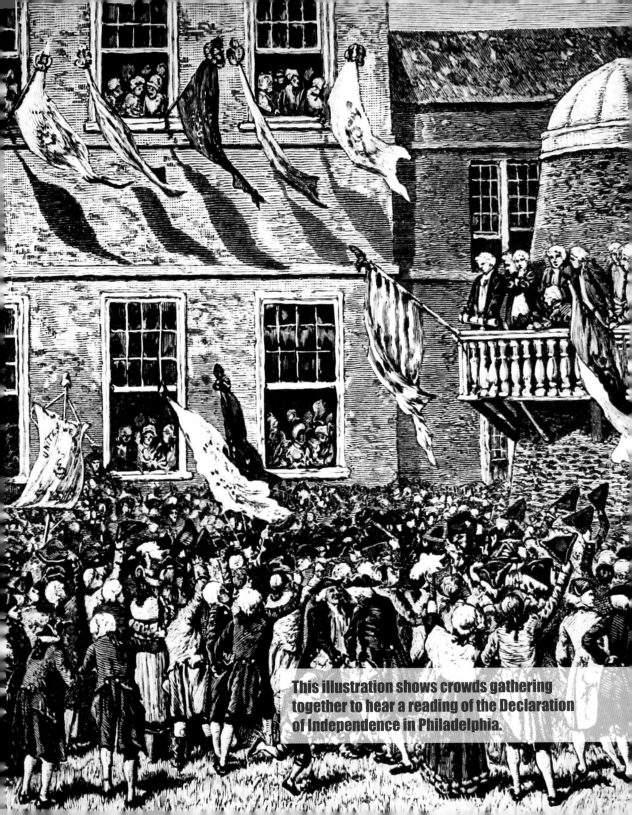

This illustration shows crowds gathering together to hear a reading of the Declaration of Independence in Philadelphia.

WORDS THAT CHANGED THE WORLD

The Second Continental Congress agreed to unite for independence with a **unanimous** vote. The Declaration of Independence was edited and presented to Congress. On July 4, 1776, this historic document was officially adopted by the new American government. The document changed the course of American history.

Independence Day

News spread about the Declaration of Independence. On July 9, 1776, George Washington addressed his troops in New York City with the news. The excited crowd tore down a statue of King George III, melted it, and made **ammunition** out of it.

Fast Fact

A total of 86 changes were made to Jefferson's original draft. These included the removal of a section speaking out against the slave trade.

Immediately after its approval of the Declaration of Independence, Congress asked Philadelphia printer John Dunlap to print about 200 copies of it. These copies, known as broadsides, were sent throughout the states and given to local leaders, newspapers, and soldiers fighting the war. One of these copies was sent to Britain as the United States' official announcement of independence. On August 2, 1776, most of the delegates signed the Declaration. They knew they were putting their lives in danger but believed they were doing the right thing.

Fast Fact

The Declaration of Independence wasn't signed until about a month after its approval. Part of this delay was because Congress was waiting for the Declaration to be "engrossed," or written clearly on parchment paper.

The next year, Philadelphia marked Independence Day on July 4. Congress established Independence Day as an official national holiday in 1870, and we still celebrate it today.

This 19th-century scene depicts Independence Day, with people celebrating around an American flag.

24

WINNING THE REVOLUTION

Americans fought British troops on the home front until the British surrender at the Battle of Yorktown on October 19, 1781. Around 6,800 American soldiers died in battle, and many more were wounded, taken prisoner, or died from disease. Two years after the formal fighting in America ended, England signed the Treaty of Paris of 1783. This was the official end to the American Revolution. Even after the war, the United States faced many tests, including creating a new government and, in time, fighting a civil war. Throughout these challenges, Americans attempted to keep alive the principles of the Declaration of Independence, including just government, basic rights, and equality.

Shown here is a depiction of the signing of the Treaty of Paris in 1783.

Equality and Democracy

The Declaration of Independence set the tone for the new nation. On November 19, 1863, President Abraham Lincoln reflected back on this document in his Gettysburg Address, saying, "Fourscore and seven years ago our fathers brought forth, on this continent, a new nation, conceived in liberty, and dedicated to the proposition that all men are created equal."

> **Fast Fact**
>
> **Thomas Jefferson and John Adams died on the same day—July 4, 1826. It was exactly 50 years after the Declaration of Independence was adopted.**

Executive Mansion,

Washington, , 186 .

Four score and seven years ago our fathers brought forth, upon this continent, a new nation, conceived in liberty, and dedicated to the proposition that "all men are created equal"

Now we are engaged in a great civil war, testing whether that nation, or any nation so conceived, and so dedicated, can long endure. We are met on a great battle field of that war. We have come to dedicate a port ... ing place for those who ... might live, This we may, in all propriety do. But, in a

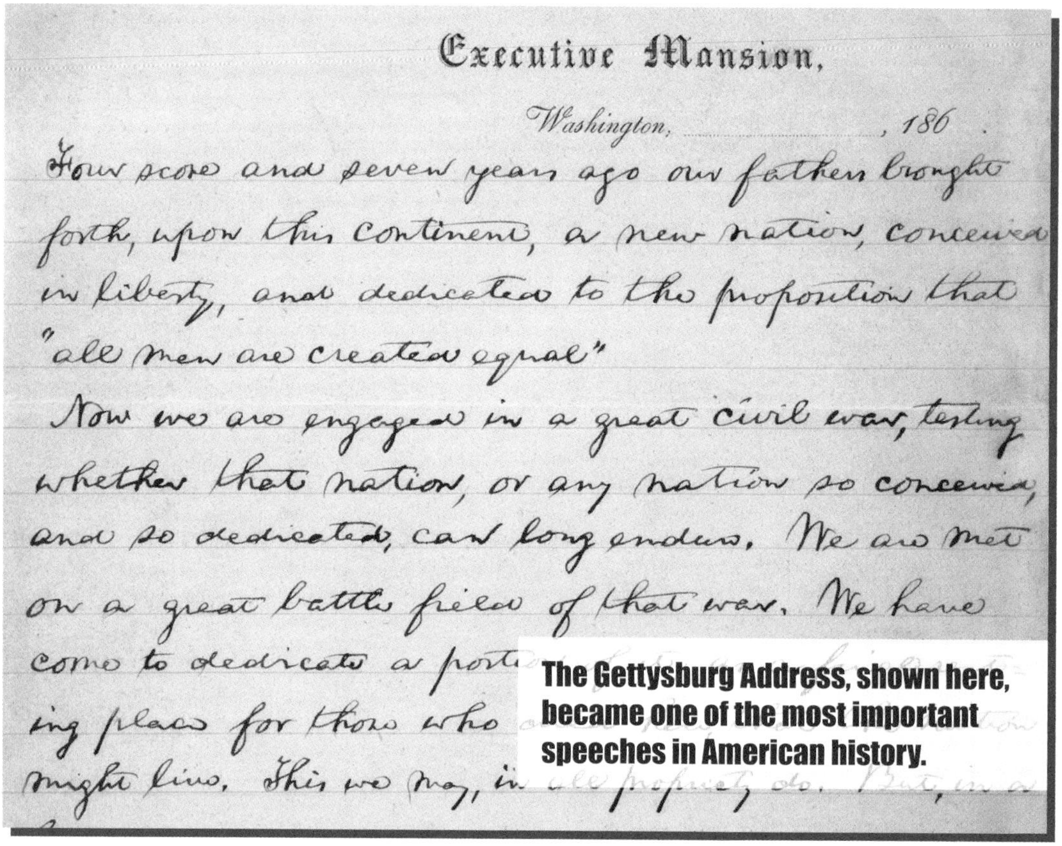

The Gettysburg Address, shown here, became one of the most important speeches in American history.

After the United States won independence, France fought its own revolutionary war. The Declaration of the Rights of Man and of the Citizen was passed in 1789 in France and can be seen here.

The ideas of equality and democracy put forth in the Declaration of Independence later helped spark cries for independence around the world, including in the Netherlands, Venezuela, and Mexican-controlled Texas. In each of these places, the new nations wrote their own declarations of independence using words and phrases similar to those in the American document. The French "Declaration of the Rights of Man and of the Citizen" was also inspired by the Declaration of Independence. Written in 1789, the French Declaration states that men have "natural, unalienable and sacred rights."

The Declaration of Independence was a revolutionary document when it was written. The Founding Fathers risked their lives to sign it, and people died on battlefields for the possibilities it presented. Today, the document is still important as it reminds Americans of the basic principles on which this country was founded.

The Declaration of Independence can be seen at the National Archives in Washington, D.C.

THE PARTS OF THE DECLARATION OF INDEPENDENCE

1 Preamble:

- ensures a "unanimous" declaration and united front by all colonies
- states that it's "necessary" to break from Britain
- declares that all men are created equal and have "unalienable" rights
- claims that when a government abuses its power, people have a right and duty to alter or abolish it

2 List of Grievances:

- lists 28 grievances, including:
  - the king's interference with colonial governments
  - the British army's occupation of colonial land during peacetime
  - taxation without consent
  - the prevention of trade with other countries
  - disregard for the colonists' right to a trial by jury

3 Declaration of Independence:

- declares that colonies are now free and independent states
- asserts that the new nation has the right to wage war and declare peace
- establishes that the new United States can form alliances with other countries
- declares that states have the full power of independent states

1. Why do you think some colonies wanted to remain loyal to Britain at first while others wanted independence?

2. Why was it important for all colonies to approve the Declaration of Independence?

3. What did the list of grievances add to the Declaration of Independence?

4. How does the Declaration of Independence affect us today?

GLOSSARY

abolish: To officially end or stop something.

ammunition: Bullets, shells, and other things fired by weapons

boycott: The act of joining with others in refusing to deal with someone or support a business as a form of protest.

civil war: A war between two opposing groups within a country.

democracy: The free and equal right of every person to participate in a government.

Enlightenment: A movement that began in the 18th century and was marked by a focus on reason and a rejection of traditional social, religious, and political ideas.

Founding Father: One of the leading figures in the founding of the United States.

grievance: A complaint.

impose: To establish or apply by authority.

militia: A group of people who are not an official part of the armed forces of a country but are trained like soldiers.

smuggler: One who takes something in and out of a country without paying duties imposed by law.

tyrant: An absolute ruler uncontrolled by laws or a constitution.

unanimous: With all members in agreement.

FIND OUT MORE

Books

Morlock, Jeremy. *Problem-Solving Methods of the Continental Congress*. New York, NY: PowerKids Press, 2019.

Murray, Laura K. *The Declaration of Independence*. North Mankato, MN: Capstone Publishing, 2020.

Redding, Anna Crowley. *Rescuing the Declaration of Independence: How We Almost Lost the Words that Built America*. New York, NY: Harper, 2020.

Websites

American Revolution
www.dkfindout.com/us/history/american-revolution/
Discover the famous documents, leaders, and events of the American Revolution.

The Declaration of Independence
www.ushistory.org/us/10g.asp
Explore the history behind the Declaration of Independence.

Thomas Jefferson
www.timeforkids.com/g56/thomas-jefferson/
Meet Thomas Jefferson—the main author of the Declaration of Independence.

INDEX